# DECADES OF THE
# 20TH
# CENTURY

# 1900s

ELDORADO INK

# DECADES OF THE 20ᵀᴴ CENTURY

1900s

1910s

1920s

1930s

1940s

1950s

1960s

1970s

1980s

1990s

# DECADES OF THE
# 20<sup>TH</sup> CENTURY

# 1900s

ELDORADO INK

Published by Eldorado Ink
2099 Lost Oak Trail
Prescott, AZ 86303
www.eldoradoink.com

Milan Bobek, Editor
Judith C. Callomon, Historical consultant
Samuel J. Patti, Consulting editor

Printed and bound in Slovenia

**Publisher Cataloging Data**

1900s / [Milan Bobek, editor].
    p. cm. -- (Decades of the 20th century)
    Includes index.
    Summary: This volume, arranged chronologically, presents key events that have shaped the decade, from significant political occurrences to details of daily life.
    ISBN 1-932904-00-X
    1. Nineteen hundreds (Decade) 2. History, Modern--20th century--Chronology 3. History, Modern--20th century--Pictorial works I. Bobek, Milan II. Title: Nineteen hundreds III. Series
    909.82/1--dc22

Picture research and photography by Anne Hobart Lang and Rolf Lang of AHL Archives. Additional research by Heritage Picture Collection, London.

# CONTENTS

# A NEW CENTURY

CHANGE is in the air as the new century begins. In Europe, alliances are changed. In Asia, Japan emerges from isolation and China enters its last imperial phase. Russia experiences its first revolution. Industry and technology grow apace in the United States. Women on both sides of the Atlantic opt for militancy in their quest for the vote. Science, too, is revolutionary: the first manned flight, wireless transmission, new plastics, psychoanalysis, relativity, and the arrival of mass-produced cars. Society is on the move.

OPPOSITE: World Exhibition opens on April 14 in Paris, France.

## 1900–1909

### KEY EVENTS OF THE DECADE

- BOER WAR
- BOXER REBELLION
- FREUD DEVELOPS PSYCHOANALYSIS
- FIRST SUCCESSFUL MANNED FLIGHT
- RUSSO-JAPANESE WAR
- WOMEN FIGHT FOR THE VOTE
- REVOLUTION IN RUSSIA
- EINSTEIN PUBLISHES THEORY OF RELATIVITY
- HORMONES ARE DISCOVERED
- RADIOACTIVITY IS EXPLAINED

- BLERIOT FLIES THE CHANNEL
- FIRST NOBEL PRIZES AWARDED
- FIRST TRANSATLANTIC RADIO TRANSMISSION
- VACUUM CLEANER INVENTED
- FORD DEVELOPS MODEL T MOTOR CAR
- PEARY REACHES NORTH POLE
- CUBISM IS BORN
- BALLETS RUSSES FOUNDED
- THE FIRST WESTERN IS SCREENED

WORLD POPULATION: 1,608 MILLION

# BOER WAR AND BOXER REBELLION

As a new century opens, conflict remains a common theme. The Boer War continues in South Africa, where the establishment of concentration camps shocks the world. In China, the Boxer uprising gives violent expression to anti-Western sentiment. In the world of science, the findings of Sigmund Freud and Max Planck revolutionize psychology and physics. In the visual world, Art Nouveau transforms the streets of Paris.

OPPOSITE: Chinese nationalist, member of the Boxer society, "Society of Harmonious Fists."

## 1 9 0 0

| | | |
|---|---|---|
| **Feb** | 9 | Dwight Davis creates Davis Cup tennis tournament |
| | 27 | Labour Party founded in U.K. |
| **Mar** | 19 | Arthur Evans begins to unearth Knossos, Crete |
| **Apr** | 14 | World Exhibition opens in Paris, France |
| **May** | 17 | British army relieves Mafeking in South Africa |
| | 20 | Second Olympic Games begin in Paris, France |
| | 31 | Boxer Rebellion breaks out in China |
| **June** | 19 | Theodore Roosevelt, hero of the Spanish-American War (1898), is nominated for U.S. vice president |
| | 24 | Boxers destroy foreign embassies in China |
| **July** | 2 | Zeppelin makes maiden flight in Germany |
| | 19 | Paris Métro opens |
| | 29 | Anarchist assassinates King Umberto of Italy |
| **Aug** | 13 | *Deutschland* wins Blue Riband as the fastest transatlantic liner |
| | 14 | Allied forces enter Peking, China |
| | 25 | Friedrich Nietzsche dies |
| **Sep** | 19 | Alfred Dreyfus pardoned in France |
| **Oct** | 14 | Sigmund Freud publishes *The Interpretation of Dreams* |
| | 26 | Britain annexes Transvaal, South Africa |
| **Nov** | 9 | Russia completes annexation of Manchuria |
| | 30 | Writer Oscar Wilde dies in exile in France |

# THE BOER WAR

Following years of tension between Britain and the Boers in South Africa, British forces under General Buller attempt to break through Boer lines in January and relieve Ladysmith. After initial successes, the British are forced to withdraw, having suffered losses of 87 officers and 1,647 men.

In February, the diamond mining town of Kimberley, which has been besieged by the Boers since October 1899 and under severe bombardment, is relieved by a British cavalry force numbering some 5,000.

The small town of Mafeking has been defended by a garrison of 700 irregulars and armed townsmen since October 1899. It is besieged by 5,000 Boers under General Cronje. The town is bombarded continuously and on May 12, 300 Boers attack and break in, but are forced to surrender. On May 17, the town is relieved by a cavalry column commanded by Colonel Mahon.

ABOVE: Crowds outside the town-hall, Cape Town, as the British decide to annex the Boer Republics.

ABOVE: Descendants of Dutch colonists, the Boers fight bitterly for control of Transvaal and Orange Free State.

ABOVE: New South Wales troops leave Sydney for South Africa. Reinforcements from the Dominions aid British victory.

ABOVE: British forces cross the Tugela river on their way to Spion Kop, where Boers force a British retreat.

RIGHT: British prisoners of war at Nooitgedacht. In retaliation for Boer guerrilla attacks, the British set up concentration camps for Boer civilians.

## BOXER REBELLION

Anti-Western sentiment explodes into revolt in China in May as the Society of Harmonious Fists, or the Boxers, assassinate the German minister and besiege foreign legations. The Boxers, who have the support of the dowager empress, are campaigning to rid China of all foreign influences. European nations, led by Britain and Germany, relieve the legations later in the year and re-establish their authority in China.

## DREAMS INTERPRETED

Sigmund Freud (1856–1939), a Moravian-born doctor working in Vienna, publishes his first major work, *The Interpretation of Dreams*. It promotes his theory, based on the study or "psychoanalysis" of his patients, that unconscious motives influence behavior. He analyzes the meaning of dreams, which are clues to unconscious memories. Freud's work will revolutionize thinking about the human psyche.

## ANARCHIST ASSASSINATES ITALIAN KING

After 22 years on the throne, Umberto I of Italy is assassinated by an anarchist in July. It is thought that he was shot in revenge for using the army to crush a revolt in Milan in 1898. Umberto is succeeded by his son, Victor Emmanuel.

ABOVE: Allied forces prepare to enter the Forbidden City, Peking, China, breaking the Boxer siege.

## POLITICAL PARTY FOR U.K. WORKERS

In Britain, representatives of the trade union movement, the Independent Labour Party (ILP), the neo-Marxist Social Democratic Federation, and the Fabian Society, a socialist think-tank, have come together to form the Labour Representation Committee (LRC) under its secretary Ramsay MacDonald, a member of the ILP. The LRC aims to increase the representation of working people in parliament and to reverse recent court judgments against trade unions.

## FIRST BOX BROWNIE

George Eastman of the United States markets his first Box Brownie roll-film camera. It costs just $1 and brings photography to the mass market.

## FIRST DAVIS CUP

American Dwight F. Davis comes up with the idea of a tennis contest between nations. He donates a silver trophy and goes on to win the first match in the competition. Davis also leads the American team to victory over Great Britain in the first Davis Cup.

ABOVE: Count Zeppelin's mighty airship moored in its shed after making its successful flight.

## ZEPPELIN TAKES TO THE AIR

Count Ferdinand von Zeppelin of Germany launches his first dirigible (steerable) airship, *LZ 1*, in July. Its flight lasts about 20 minutes.

## U.S. GOLD STANDARD

President McKinley signs into law a bill that puts the United States on the gold standard. Any future money, either printed or coined, will be backed by an equal amount of gold held in reserve by the U.S. Treasury.

## METRO TRANSFORMS PARIS

Art Nouveau architect Hector Guimard transforms the streets of Paris with his entrances to the new Paris Métro. He uses iron and glass in new ways, which are both beautiful in their use of whiplash curves, plant-like forms and distinctive typography, but also highly practical. The roof panels, for instance, are standardized for ease of manufacture.

## PETER RABBIT IS BORN

This year sees the writing of *The Tale of Peter Rabbit*, the first of a series of children's stories by English author Beatrix Potter (1866–1943). First published privately, *Peter Rabbit* becomes a firm favorite and will be followed by many similar volumes, which remain popular throughout the century. The use of the author's own illustrations and a small format, perfectly suited for children's hands, make this a highly influential book.

## TOSCA TAKES THE STAGE

Giacomo Puccini's opera *Tosca* is performed. The full-blooded melodies, violent action, tense emotions, and vivid characters of Puccini's work take traditional Italian opera just about as far as it can go. Puccini is also the chief exponent of the *verismo* or realism style. His plot is so dramatic that audiences can tell what is going on from the music and action, without understanding the language.

## MINOAN DISCOVERY

British archaeologist Arthur Evans (1851–1941) uncovers Knossos, capital of the Bronze Age Minoan civilization on the Aegean island of Crete. His remarkable discoveries include the magnificent palace of the legendary King Minos and pottery fragments decorated with Minoan script.

## LORD JIM

Author Joseph Conrad's first great novel, *Lord Jim*, launches the Polish exile on his path. His awareness of the power of evil and how idealism can be corrupted make him a major figure in fiction.

ABOVE: An imposing stairway leads to the Java Pavilion at the World Exhibition, Paris.

## PAPER CLIP

The paper clip is patented in Germany by its Norwegian inventor, Johann Vaaler. Before its invention, papers are fastened together with pins.

## PLUNGER SUBMERGES

American inventor John Holland has added further refinements to his submersible, the *Plunger*. The first streamlined submersible to be built, it is propelled by electricity when submerged (it was previously steam-driven on the surface). Now Holland has replaced the steam engine with a more efficient gasoline engine.

The invaluable paper clip.

## CONCENTRATION CAMPS

British troops conquer the Transvaal and Orange Free State in November and scatter the Boer armies. The British are beginning to intern Boer women and children in concentration camps to prevent them helping Boer soldiers. This move causes an international outrage.

ABOVE: Fashionable shooting outfit for sporting women.

## MCKINLEY AGAIN

President and republican incumbent William McKinley was reelected along with vice presidential candidate Theodore Roosevelt. William Jennings Bryan of Nebraska was defeated by McKinley for the second time in four years. The republicans also increased their majority in both the House and Senate.

## CAKEWALK

A strutting dance, the cakewalk, which originated among black American slaves, hits Europe's dance halls.

## DARING SWIMSUIT

Annette Kellerman, American aquatic star, introduces the one-piece swimsuit.

## SECOND OLYMPICS

The second of the modern Olympic Games is held in Paris, France, from May to October, to coincide with the World Exhibition. However, events are scattered over six months and across northern France, diluting public interest. In contrast to the all-male games of 1896, women compete in a limited number of events.

## THE QUANTUM THEORY

German physicist Max Planck (1858–1947) of Berlin University discovers that energy consists of basic units, each of which he calls quanta. This marks the beginning of quantum theory, revolutionizes the study of physics, and wins him a 1918 Nobel Prize.

## RADIOACTIVE GAS

German physicist Friedrich Ernst Dorn discovers the dangerous radioactive gas radon, the sixth of the "noble gases." He finds it emanating from a sample of radium.

## THE WORLD EXHIBITS IN PARIS

The world's most innovative technology goes on exhibition in Paris, France. The Palace of Electricity, illuminated at night, and escalators from the United States show how the new century will transform daily life. The Rodin Pavilion, France's major exhibit, is a celebration of the great sculptor.

### OSCAR WILDE
### (1854–1900)

The once-flamboyant Irish writer and brilliant epigramist, Oscar Wilde dies in France aged 44. Author of *The Importance of Being Earnest* and *The Picture of Dorian Gray*, Wilde was imprisoned for homosexual offenses in 1895. He served a two year prison sentence, which he described in *The Ballad of Reading Gaol*.

## YELLOW FEVER

An American army doctor, Walter Reed, discovers that the deadly disease yellow fever is transmitted by mosquitoes. He does this by studying the disease in Cuba with the help of human volunteers. Eliminating the mosquitoes in Panama later enables engineers to construct the Panama Canal.

## GAMMA RAYS

French physicist Paul Ulrich Villard discovers that radium puts out a third kind of radiation, in addition to the alpha rays and beta rays already discovered. These new electromagnetic rays are later named gamma rays.

## ENTER ELECTRONS

French physicist Henri Becquerel (1852–1908) discovers that the radioactivity from the element radium consists of the subatomic particles, electrons. He also finds that radioactivity can cause one element to change into another.

## SISTER CARRIE

The highly realistic novel, *Sister Carrie*, by American master Theodore Dreiser, is effectively suppressed by the publishers because of its alleged immorality when "sin" is not "punished." The book is published, but not publicized.

ABOVE: A Chinese passport signed by statesman Li Hung Chang. A pro-Westerner, Li Hung Chang promoted links with Europe, which were resented by the Boxers.

ABOVE: Severe flooding in Rome creates an unusual image of the Forum.

# RADIO, TORPEDOES, AND NOBEL PRIZES

Europen and Commonwealth countries mourn the death of Queen Victoria. She had reigned for 64 years, giving her name to a particular and remarkable period of history - the Victorian Age. As if to mark the start of a new era, the first-ever transatlantic radio signal is transmitted successfully and a black American is honored at the White House for the first time.

OPPOSITE: British sailors prepare to draw Queen Victoria's coffin through the streets of London.

# 1901

| | | | | | |
|---|---|---|---|---|---|
| **Jan** | 1 | Commonwealth of Australia comes into being | **Sep** | 7 | Peking Treaty ends the Boxer Rising in China |
| | 10 | Oil is discovered in Texas | | 9 | Artist Toulouse-Lautrec dies. |
| | 22 | Death of Queen Victoria in U.K. | | 14 | President McKinley dies from a gun shot wound received on Sept. 6. Vice President Theodore Roosevelt is sworn in as the new President |
| **Feb** | 26 | Boxer leaders are publicly executed in China | | | |
| **Mar** | 1 | First monorail is opened in Wuppertal, Germany | **Oct** | 4 | The American yacht Columbia retains America's Cup by defeating the British challenger Shamrock |
| | 4 | President Mckinley is inaugurated for his second term in office | | 16 | Black American Booker T. Washington dines at White House |
| | 13 | First Mercedes is built by Daimler in Germany | | | |
| | 17 | Students riot in Russia | **Nov** | 18 | The United States is granted the rights by the U.K. to build a neutral canal through Central America |
| **June** | 24 | Unknown artist Pablo Picasso exhibits for the first time | | | |
| | | | **Dec** | 10 | First Nobel Prizes awarded |
| **Aug** | 4 | Gold is discovered in Rand, South Africa | | 12 | Marconi sends first transatlantic wireless message |

ABOVE: U.S. President McKinley and his cabinet at the White House.

## U.S. PRESIDENT ASSASSINATED

President William McKinley is shot and killed in Buffalo, New York, by Polish anarchist Leon Czolgosz in a September protest against the American government. Vice president Theodore Roosevelt is on a climbing holiday when he hears the news and is sworn in as the 26th president at the age of 42.

## FIRST TRANSATLANTIC RADIO

Worldwide radio communication becomes possible when the first transatlantic radio signal, the morse letter "S", is transmitted. A team working for the Italian pioneer of radio, Guglielmo Marconi (1874–1937), sends the signal from Poldhu, Cornwall, in the U.K. to St. John's, Newfoundland, on December 12.

## MEN IN THE MOON

Creator of science fiction, author H.G. Wells, anticipates the future with his new novel *The First Men in the Moon*. The spirit of adventure, the explanation of technology, and the conquest of space are themes which will recur in science fiction of later decades.

## EUROPEAN ELEMENT

French chemist Eugène Dumarçay discovers the rare earth element europium, which he names in honor of Europe.

## END OF AN ERA

Queen Victoria dies at the age of 82. She has ruled Britain since 1837 and seen it grow into the most powerful economic and military power in the world, with a vast empire on every continent. Through her children and grandchildren, she is related to every monarch in Europe and her funeral is attended by heads of state from around the world.

## BLACK AMERICAN AT THE WHITE HOUSE

President Theodore Roosevelt (1858–1919) entertains black American Booker T. Washington at dinner in the White House, the first black man to be so honored. Booker T. Washington is a noted reformer and educator and president of the first university for blacks in the United States in Tuskegee, Alabama. Two weeks later, 34 people are killed in race riots which break out in the American South in protest to the visit.

LEFT: Luxurious dining facilities for passengers on the Paris-Lyon-Mediterranean railway.

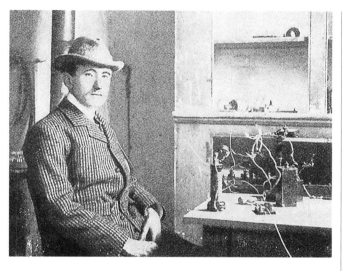

ABOVE: Marconi with his radio receiving set.

## THREE SISTERS

Konstantin Stanislavsky directs Anton Chekhov's play, *The Three Sisters*, written especially for the Moscow Art Theatre, in a milestone production that brings him fame. His insistence on a permanent, high-quality company of actors, his enthusiasm for a realistic acting style, and his belief in the theatre as a means of educating people, later find expression in the Method style of acting, in which the actor draws on his or her past experiences in creating a role.

## MORO WARS BREAK OUT

Violence breaks out in the Philippines when the United States, in control of the Philippines since 1898, demands that the Moros, Muslim tribespeople, assimilate with Christian islanders.

BELOW: Loading an aerial torpedo - a new and deadly weapon.

ABOVE: Motor racing gains popularity; here a French contestant reaches Berlin.

## BLOOD GROUPS

Viennese-born U.S. immunologist Karl Landsteiner discovers that blood can be categorized into three groups, A, B and O, a method of sorting still used today. Landsteiner later discovers a fourth group, AB.

## VACUUM CLEANER INVENTED

Herbert Cecil Booth, an English civil engineer, invents the vacuum cleaner. His first machine is mounted on a horse-drawn cart and powered by a gasoline engine. Long tubes are passed into houses to clean them.

## MUTATIONS

Dutch botanist Hugo de Vries, who in 1900 rediscovered Gregor Mendel's laws of heredity, discovers that new forms of plants can arise suddenly and gives this process the name "mutation." He introduces the experimental method of studying plant evolution.

## MERCURY LAMP

American electrical engineer Peter Cooper-Hewitt markets the mercury vapor electric arc lamp. It produces a light that is nearly shadow-free.

## BUDDENBROOKS

German author Thomas Mann (1875–1955) publishes his first novel, *Buddenbrooks*. In it, Mann portrays the decline of one German family. They lose their money, their creativity, and their very will to live, using this as a symbol for the decline of Germany itself.

## WOMEN STUDENTS ENTER ROCHESTER

American feminist Susan B. Anthony persuades Rochester University, New York, to accept women students. She raises nearly $100,000 to pay the tuition costs.

## SHAVING TIME

The first safety razor with throwaway blades is made by King Camp Gillette of Boston, Massachusetts. For two years he has to give the razors away until he can find a backer to set him up with a factory. By 1908, he is selling 14 million blades a year.

## SALOON BUSTER

American temperance agitator Carry Nation continues her campaign for the closure of saloons. At 6 feet tall, she arms herself with a hatchet and is accompanied by hymn-singing followers when she goes saloon-busting.

## ANTARCTIC EXPEDITION

Robert Falcon Scott, commander of the British National Antarctic Expedition, sets sail in the *Discovery* from New Zealand. The expedition explores the Ross Sea area, sighting the Transantarctic Mountains, reaching the polar plateau and discovering Taylor Valley.

LEFT: Workmen strengthen wires on the Brooklyn Bridge, the world's largest suspension bridge, crossing the East River, in New York City.

LEFT: *Shamrock II*, challenger for the America's Cup.

RIGHT: Dunlop is the latest in pneumatic bicycle tires.

## FIRST NOBEL PRIZES

The first-ever Nobel Prizes for achievements in physics, chemistry, medicine or physiology, literature, and peace are awarded. They were endowed in 1895 by Alfred Nobel, the Swedish chemist and inventor of dynamite. Jacobus Henricus van't Hoff (Holland) is awarded the prize in chemistry for his work on thermodynamics and stereochemistry. Wilhelm Roentgen (Germany) receives the physics prize for his discovery of X-rays. Sully Prudhomme (France) receives the literature prize, Jean-Henri Dunant (Switzerland), founder of the Red Cross, and Frédéric Passy (France) jointly receive the peace prize.

## AUSTRALIAN COMMONWEALTH

The Commonwealth of Australia comes into being in January. The six former Australian colonies are now united within a single federal state, but there are already difficulties over nonwhite immigration and the growing demands of the trade union and labor movement for better working conditions.

## ANTI-SEMITISM IN RUSSIA

Anti-Semitism drives many Russian Jews to Palestine to settle in farming colonies set up by Baron Rothschild.

BELOW: Excavation for the western channel of the massive Nile dam being built in Egypt.

## ROCKEFELLER INSTITUTE FOUNDED

American philanthropist and oil magnate, John D. Rockefeller, founds the Rockefeller Institute for Medical Research.

## CHRISTMAS TREES ARE LIT UP

Christmas tree lights are among the ideas developed by the Edison General Electric Co. The business was founded by inventor Thomas Edison in 1889.

# TEDDY BEAR DEBUT

The Treaty of Vereeniging brings an end to the Boer War, the Japanese and British enter a formal alliance, and France and Italy sign an *entente*. Hormones are discovered and surgery makes a major advance when the technique of suturing is developed. Italian tenor Enrico Caruso becomes the world's first recording star and American president "Teddy" Roosevelt gives his name to what will become one of the world's favorite toys.

## 1902

| | | |
|---|---|---|
| Jan | 7 | Chinese imperial court returns to Peking after suppression of Boxer uprising |
| | 30 | Britain and Japan sign peace treaty |
| Feb | 1 | Footbinding outlawed in China |
| Mar | 26 | Cecil Rhodes, architect of imperialism, dies |
| May | 31 | Treaty of Vereeniging ends the Boer War |
| June | 28 | Congress authorizes the spending of $40,000,000 for land rights to build the Panama Canal |
| Sep | 29 | French novelist Emile Zola (b. 1840) dies |
| Nov | 1 | Franco-Italian *entente* |

ABOVE: Russian novelist and visionary Leo Tolstoy (1828–1910), famed for his novels and rejection of materialism.

## BOER WAR ENDS
At Vereeniging, South Africa, Britain and the Boer leaders finally sign a peace treaty in May. It marks the end of the Boer War, which has lasted for nearly three years. The Boers are forced to accept British colonial rule, with a promise of self-government later, and a substantial grant of £3 million to help rebuild their shattered countries.

## VOTES FOR ALL IN AUSTRALIA
Australia grants universal suffrage, allowing women aged 21 and over to vote in federal elections with the same rights as men. This follows New Zealand's example in granting universal suffrage, which is unknown throughout Europe and the United States.

## JAPANESE-BRITISH ALLIANCE
Britain and Japan sign a treaty of alliance in January, by which both agree not to make a treaty with a third country without the other's consent. The agreement safeguards Britain's interests in China and Japan's interests in Korea and is the first alliance Britain has signed for many years.

ABOVE: Despite appalling conditions in the camps, Boer prisoners maintain their spirits with amateur dramatics.

## A TRIP TO THE MOON
Georges Méliès's latest film, *A Voyage to the Moon*, opens to acclaim. Using innovative special effects and combining magic and fantasy, it consists of 30 scenes and will bring Méliès, a conjurer by training, international fame.

## FIRST TEDDY BEAR
Russian-born Morris Michton, a New York candy store assistant, makes the world's first teddy bear. He was inspired by a Clifford Berryman cartoon in the *Washington Evening Star* which showed President "Teddy" Roosevelt on a hunting trip, refusing to shoot a mother bear.

## STITCHES IN TIME
French surgeon Alexis Carrel develops the technique of suturing blood vessels (arteries and veins) together end to end. It is a major development in surgery.

## TOP OF THE CHARTS

Italian tenor Enrico Caruso (1873–1921) becomes the first recording star when he makes ten records for the Victor company. They include "Vesti la giubba" from *Pagliacci*, which will eventually become the first classical record to sell one million copies.

## FRANCO-ITALIAN ENTENTE

France and Italy sign an *entente* in which Italy assures France of its neutrality if France is attacked. The French government is increasingly concerned by the growing military and economic might of Germany and is thus ensuring the security of its border with Italy.

## RIYADH RECAPTURED

Abdul Aziz ibn Abdul Rahman of the al Saud family recaptures Riyadh from the Turks following a series of campaigns against the Turks and other family groups.

## EARLY MORNING TEA

Frank Clarke, a gunsmith from Birmingham, England, makes the first automatic tea-maker. It is powered by clockwork, strikes a match to light a spirit stove, and pours boiling water into a teapot. It then sets off a bedside alarm.

## FLATIRON BUILDING

Daniel H. Burnham's twenty-story Flatiron Building in New York City, with its slim lines tapering to almost nothing, shows for the first time how modern concrete and steel technology gives the architect scope to create new shapes and forms.

## DISASTER IN AFRICA

On the French ruled island of Martinique, West Africa, the volcano Mount Pele erupts. Some 30,000 people are killed.

ABOVE: Franz Josef, Emperor of Austria. His attack on Serbia in 1914 precipitates World War I.

RIGHT: King Edward VII of Britain and Queen Alexandra on board the royal yacht *Victoria and Albert*.

ABOVE: Four years in the making, the Nile dam is completed.

## PHOTO-SECESSION GROUP

This group of photographers, based in New York City, is led by Alfred Stieglitz and Edward Steichen. They uphold the right of the photographer to be considered an artist and publish the influential photographic journal, *Camera Work*, which will run until 1917.

## CORONATION DAY

Rulers of Europe gather in London for the coronation of Edward VII on August 9. The coronation has been postponed from June when Edward was forced to undergo an emergency operation for appendicitis. The king, who is 60, has made a good recovery in time for the coronation and the many diplomatic and public events associated with it.

## HORMONES DISCOVERED

British physicists Ernest Henry Starling and William Bayliss discover that secretin, produced in the duodenum, acts on another organ of the body, the pancreas. Three years later they name this and other substances "hormones."

## FOOT BINDING BANNED

The binding of the feet of Han Chinese women is banned in China by imperial edict after petitions from reform groups. The first reform group was founded in Canton in 1894 and was followed by others in provincial capitals.

## IONOSPHERE SUGGESTED

British physicist Oliver Heaviside suggests that a layer of electrical charges in the atmosphere might be reflecting wireless waves back to Earth. Simultaneously, Arthur Edwin Kennelly of the United States puts forward the same idea. It is proved 20 years later and is now called the ionosphere.

## HEART OF DARKNESS

Joseph Conrad (1857–1924) publishes his novel *Heart of Darkness*. It portrays a journey into the interior of Africa, where Conrad himself had travelled. He brings to life the terrifying consequences of human corruptibility in a colonial setting.

## PELLEAS ET MELISANDE

Creator of musical impressionism, Claude Debussy (1862–1918) premieres his only completed opera, *Pelléas et Mélisande*. In this work, Debussy evokes a nightmarish atmosphere influenced by the ghost stories of American writer Edgar Allan Poe.

## MOWING MADE EASY

The first commercially successful motorized mower is made in Britain. It is driven by a gasoline engine.

---

### ELIZABETH CADY STANTON
### (1815–1902)

The American feminist, Elizabeth Cady Stanton, dies at 87. In 1848, with the pacifist and antislavery campaigner Lucretia Mott, she launched the American women's rights movement at the Seneca Falls convention. She campaigned for sexual equality throughout her life and in 1869, with Susan B. Anthony, founded the National Woman Suffrage Association. She acted as president of the Association until 1892. In later life, she completed three of the six volumes of *History of Woman Suffrage* (1881–86), with Lucretia Mott and Matilda Joslyn Gage, and her autobiography.

# TROUBLE BREWS IN THE BALKANS

Trouble breaks out in the Balkans, where thousands of Bulgarians are massacred. In North America, the U.S. and Canadian border is finally settled and in South America, Panama achieves independence. Women in Britain adopt militancy as the best means of achieving the vote and Marie Curie becomes the first woman to receive a Nobel Prize. Color photography is developed and France's first Tour de France bicycle race takes place.

## 1903

| | | |
|---|---|---|
| Feb | 24 | British forces march against "Mad" Mullah Mohammed bin Abdullah |
| Apr | 16 | Jews massacred in Bessarabia |
| June | 15 | Cinema audiences flock to *The Great Train Robbery* |
| July | 19 | First Tour de France finishes |
| Aug | 2 | Uprising begins in Macedonia |
| Sep | 8 | Turks massacre Bulgarians |
| Oct | 10 | Women's Social and Political Union (WSPU) is founded in the U.K. |
| | 13 | Boston defeats Pittsburgh in the first World Series |
| | 20 | Alaskan boundary is decided |
| Dec | 17 | Wright brothers make first successful flight |

ABOVE: Scott's ship *Discovery* sails south from New Zealand on the Antarctic expedition. On board is a junior officer, Ernest Shackleton.

OPPOSITE: Macedonian revolutionaries dance around a campfire, while their priest looks on.

## JEWISH POGROM

Many Jews are killed by local people in the town of Kishinev, Bessarabia, in southwest Russia. The police and government turn a blind eye to the pogrom, which started on Easter Sunday. The government has been persecuting Jews since Czar Nicholas came to the throne in 1894.

## BOLSHEVIKS BREAK AWAY

At its congress in London in August, the Russian Social Democratic Party splits between the moderate Mensheviks (minority), led by G.V. Plekhanov, and the more radical Bolsheviks (majority), led by V.I. Lenin. The split harms the effectiveness of the opposition to the government of Czar Nicholas II.

## DEEDS NOT WORDS

Mrs. Emmeline Pankhurst (1857–1928) and other women meet in Manchester, U.K., to form a new women's suffrage society, the Women's Social and Political Union (WSPU). Their aim is the achievement of votes for women "by any means." In contrast to previous women suffragist groups, the WSPU takes a militant approach. Soon, they will be known as suffragettes.

## FIRST SUCCESSFUL AIRPLANE FLIGHT

Two brothers, Wilbur and Orville Wright from Ohio, achieve the first successful heavier-than-air-flight in December at Kitty Hawk, North Carolina. Their machine, the *Flyer*, flies a distance of about 120 feet. Orville is at the controls while the plane makes its first flight.

## FIRST WESTERN

Edwin S. Porter's film, *The Great Train Robbery*, is the first U.S. feature film and the first western. It marks the start of a major genre in American popular culture.

## RADIUM PRIZE

French scientists Marie and Pierre Curie, with Henri Becquerel, share the Nobel Prize for Physics, by discovering the radioactive elements radium and polonium. Marie Curie (1867–1934) is the first woman to receive a Nobel award.

## MEASURING THE HEART

The first electrocardiograph to measure heart beats is made by the Dutch physiologist Willem Einthoven at Leyden University. He uses a simple galvanometer.

BELOW: Scott's Antarctic expedition of 1901–1904. The sledge party, photographed by Shackleton, sets out from winter quarters towards the South Pole.

## BULGARIANS MASSACRED

In Macedonia, the Turkish army massacres more than 50,000 men, women, and children in its continuing action against separatists in Macedonia. The victims, who are all Bulgarian, are killed by the Turks in their campaign to prevent Bulgaria expanding its territory into Turkish-held Macedonia.

## BORDER DECISION

The commission set up to decide the frontier between Alaska and Canada finally agrees on the borderline. The decision of the British representative to favor Alaska infuriates the Canadian government.

## FIRST TOUR DE FRANCE

Maurice Garin becomes the winner on July 19 in the first ever Tour de France cycling race, which lasted for 16 days. The early years of the competition feature marathon stages, often completed in darkness.

## SAFETY RAZOR

The safety razor is patented in Boston, Massachusetts, by King Camp Gillette in association with William Nickerson, a mechanic.

## PANAMA DECLARES INDEPENDENCE

In November, the province of Panama declares its independence from Colombia in protest at delays by Colombia in agreeing to the route for the proposed Panama Canal. In December, a treaty between Panama and the United States sets up the Canal Zone, which is handed over to the United States.

## THE WAY OF ALL FLESH

This semi-autobiographical novel by Samuel Butler is published after his death. It shows the deadening influence of tradition and family on life and forms part of the reaction against Victorian views and values that is currently taking place.

## THE CALL OF THE WILD

This year sees the publication of *The Call of the Wild* by Jack London. The story is about a dog, Buck, who leads a pack of wolves after his master dies. It becomes one of the most popular novels by this socialist writer.

## HEADACHE REMEDY

The painkiller, aspirin, is launched by the German drug company A.G. Bayer.

## EXPLAINING RADIOACTIVITY

British scientists Ernest Rutherford (1871–1937) and Frederick Soddy, working in Canada, discover that radioactivity is the result of the breakdown of atoms in a radioactive element, producing a new element. They publish this as *The Cause and Nature of Radioactivity*.

## VIKING EXCAVATION

The Oseberg longship, found buried inside a peat mound overlooking a Norwegian fjord near Oslo, is excavated. Interred inside it are two women who may have been ninth century Viking nobles. As well as the women, the longship contains magnificent sledges, carts, furniture, kitchen utensils and textiles.

### PAUL GAUGUIN (1848–1903)

Paul Gauguin, the French Post-Impressionist painter, has died. In 1883 Gauguin abandoned his stockbroker career in Paris to become a painter in Brittany. His best known work was inspired by the art and culture of the South Pacific, where he lived from 1891. His primitive, exotic and dreamlike style (known as Synthesist) is seen in paintings such as *No Te Aha De Riri* (1896), and *Faa Iheihe, Decorated with Ornaments* (1898).

## SALIVATING RESPONSE

Russian psychologist Ivan Pavlov (1849–1936) reports that ringing a bell will make a hungry dog salivate, if the bell has always been rung just before the dog's food arrives. Pavlov calls this a "conditioned reflex."

## AMSTERDAM STOCK EXCHANGE

H.P. Berlage's reconstruction of the Amsterdam Stock Exchange, destroyed by fire in 1885, is completed. Based on a grid plan, the building is important for its use of red brick with a glass and metal roof.

## FIRST CONES

The first ice cream cone made of waffle pastry is patented by Italo Marcioni, an ice cream salesman in New Jersey. The cones will be introduced at the Louisiana Purchase Exposition in St. Louis in 1904.

## COLOR PHOTOGRAPHY

Louis and Auguste Lumière of France perfect the first single-plate process for color photography. It will be marketed in 1907 as Autochrome.

### PULITZER PRIZE

Joseph Pulitzer, a Hungarian-born American newspaper proprietor, once a journalist on the German-language *Westliche Post*, donates $2 million to found a school of journalism at Columbia University. He endows annual prizes for journalism. The first prizes will be awarded in 1917.

### WORLD SERIES

The Boston Pilgrims win the first baseball World Series in the United States. Boston are champions of the American League, formed in 1901, and beat the Pittsburgh Pirates, the champions of the more established National League.

ABOVE: The splendor of the Raj. Indian princes, Bengal lancers, and others parade into Delhi to proclaim Edward VII Emperor of India.

### HOMOSEXUAL SURVEY

Berlin's Scientific-Humanitarian Committee, the world's first organization for homosexual rights, founded in 1898, questions more than 6,000 students and factory workers and concludes that 2.2 per cent of the general population is homosexual.

### TIME FLIES

French magazine *Temps* sends a telegram around the world in six hours.

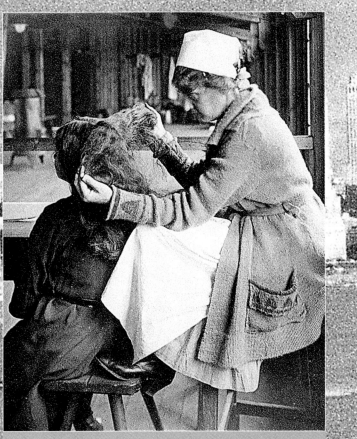

ABOVE: Emigration often provided the only means of escape for persecuted Eastern Europeans.

BELOW: Ellis Island is the first port of call for immigrants reaching the United States.

# RUSSIA TAKES ON JAPAN

Japan, having emerged from centuries of isolation, and Russia, bent on eastward expansion, clash over conflicting ambitions in Manchuria and Korea and finally go to war. By contrast, Britain and France bring to an end centuries of hostility when they sign an *entente cordiale*. In the United States, immigration figures soar as Eastern Europeans fleeing persecution flood into the country. The opening of Schlesinger-Meyer in Chicago heralds the arrival of the twentieth century department store.

## 1904

| | | |
|---|---|---|
| **Feb** | 8 | Russo-Japanese War breaks out |
| **Apr** | 8 | Britain and France sign The Entente Cordiale |
| | 13 | Japanese torpedo boats sink the battleship *Petropavlovsk* at Port Arthur |
| | 30 | World Exhibition opens in St. Louis |
| **May** | 1 | Japanese army defeats Russians at Xinyizhou |
| | 2 | Japanese fleet blocks Port Arthur |
| | 26 | Russian forces land in Manchuria |
| **July** | 1 | Olympic Games open in St. Louis |
| | 15 | Russian author Anton Chekhov (b.1860) dies |
| | 31 | Trans-Siberian Railway is completed and stretches 4607 miles |
| **Nov** | 8 | President Theodore Roosevelt is reelected |

# THE RUSSO-JAPANESE WAR

In 1903, the Japanese had proposed that the Japanese and Russian governments should safeguard each other's special economic interests in Manchuria and Korea. Angered by the Russian lack of commitment, the Japanese ambassador broke off negotiations. In February 1904, 16 Japanese warships under Admiral Togo attack a fleet of six Russian battleships and ten cruisers under Vice Admiral Stark, off Port Arthur. Japanese torpedo boats severely damage two battleships and a cruiser. Others are also damaged and the two countries are at war. In April, Japanese torpedo boats sink the Russian battleship *Petropavlovsk*. In May, Japanese ships penetrate Port Arthur and block the harbor.

In August, the Russian fleet, trapped in Port Arthur and under fire from land batteries, fights to reach the open sea. The Japanese fleet under Togo blocks their exit and forces them back into the harbor.

RIGHT: The Chinese governor of SanSin being carried ashore.

FAR RIGHT: Japanese soldiers execute traitors.

LEFT: Russian troops keep a careful lookout for Japanese from a treetop vantage point.

After a year of fighting, Russia surrenders Port Arthur to the Japanese in January. Japanese losses are 58,000 killed or wounded, and 30,000 sick.

In May, the Russian Baltic fleet, including seven battleships and six cruisers, meets a Japanese force of the same size but with greater fire-power and speed in the battle of Tsu Shima. During the afternoon of May 27, the Japanese sink four Russian battleships, damage one, and suffer no losses. The Russians attempt to escape to Vladivostok, but the Japanese destroyers and torpedo boats attack in the night and sink three ships. The battle continues the following day until all but 12 of the Russian fleet are captured, driven aground or sunk.

In September, Russia and Japan finally sign a peace treaty ending the Russo-Japanese War. The treaty marks the first time a European power is defeated in war by an Asian nation.

ABOVE: Siege guns, captured by the Japanese in August 1904, being moved by train before the battle of Liao Yang.

RIGHT: Russian troops inflate a balloon at Mukdon in 1905. The Russians were completely routed.

## ANTON CHEKOV (1860–1904)

This year sees the death of the Russian writer Anton Chekov, whose dramatic voice was so quintessentially Russian and yet universal in its appeal. Also a doctor, he was the author of 13 volumes of short stories, as well as the widely performed plays *The Seagull* (1896), *Uncle Vanya* (1900), *The Three Sisters* (1901), *The Cherry Orchard* (1904), and others. In 1897, suffering from tuberculosis, he went to live in the Crimea and died in Yalta.

## ENTENTE CORDIALE

Britain and France sign the Anglo-French Entente Cordiale, ending centuries of hostility between the two countries. The Entente settles long-standing colonial disputes between the two countries in North America, Africa, and the Pacific, and continues the British policy of seeking alliances to secure its global interests.

## INTERNATIONAL WOMEN'S SUFFRAGE

Veteran American feminist Susan B. Anthony (1820–1906), together with suffrage leader Carrie Catt, founds the International Woman Suffrage Alliance in Berlin.

## FIRST LABOUR P.M.

John Watson becomes prime minister of Australia, the first time a Labour politician has led a government anywhere in the world. He holds power only until August, when his government falls and is replaced by a coalition.

## IMMIGRATION SOARS

Competitive cuts in steerage rates by rival steamship companies stimulates Eastern European immigration into the States. Slavs, Slovaks, Serbs, Croats, Bosnians, Herzegovinians, and many Jewish immigrants fleeing persecution begin to dominate the immigrant figures.

## DIESEL-POWERED SUBMARINE

Maxim Laubeuf of France builds a diesel-powered submarine, the *Aigret*. Its lower flashpoint makes it safer than a gasoline-powered submarine.

## GIVE MY REGARDS TO BROADWAY

American musical *Little Johnny Jones* includes this song, which becomes a smash hit and sums up the importance of Broadway and its musicals in the national identity of the United States.

## PAIN RELIEF

Organic chemist Albert Einhorn of Germany first produces procaine, also known as Novocaine, which acts as a local anesthetic. It can be used instead of the more dangerous cocaine.

## PETER PAN

Scottish dramatist J.M. Barrie's new play *Peter Pan*, with its forever-young hero, Lost Boys, and Never Never Land, becomes an abiding success. Barrie follows it up with a story (1906) and a book (1911).

## JEAN-CHRISTOPHE

French author Romain Rolland (1866–1944) publishes the first of his 10 volume novel, *Jean-Christophe*, a long study of a fictional musician. Socialist, idealist, and pacifist, Rolland is important for bringing these values into fiction. He will later win the Nobel Prize in 1915.

## CHICAGO DEPARTMENT STORE

One of the finest examples of an early twentieth century department store is Louis Sullivan's Schlesinger-Meyer. Sullivan's style combines rich ornament on the lower floors with modern steel, glass, and concrete construction. The building also includes public rooms such as an art gallery, restaurant, and lounge.

## NONFLAMMABLE CELLULOID

French chemists produce a nonflammable version of celluloid by adding metallic salts during manufacture. This spoils the old joke about the readiness of celluloid to burn: "Please do not smoke as I am wearing a celluloid collar."

## ELECTRIC EYE

The first practical photo-electric cell, also called the "electric eye," is invented by Johann Elster of Germany. In the same year, German professor Arthur Korn uses one to transmit a picture over a telegraph wire.

ABOVE: The wrecked pleasure steamer *General Slocum* lies in New York harbor after a fire costing the lives of 1,000 passengers.

ABOVE: Pilgrims flood into Jerusalem to celebrate Christmas.

### ABBEY THEATRE FOUNDED
Irish poet W.B. Yeats and Augusta, Lady Gregory (later joined by J.M. Synge as co-director) found the Abbey Theatre in Dublin. The theatre will be identified with a renaissance in Irish culture and many of the important twentieth century Irish plays will be premiered there.

### JUPITER SATELLITE
U.S. astronomer Charles Dillon Perrine discovers Himalia, the sixth satellite of the planet Jupiter.

### ST. LOUIS OLYMPICS
The Olympic Games take place in St. Louis at the same time as the World Exhibition. Crowds flock to the Exhibition but, as in 1900, the unfocused games fail to attract large crowds. European involvement is limited because of the cost of travel. Only 680 athletes take part, 500 of whom are American or Canadian.

### GIBSON GIRL
Charles Dana Gibson, a New York illustrator with a reputation for capturing aristocratic ideals, creates the Gibson Girl, an elegant beauty. His inspiration is his wife Irene Langhorne, whose fresh-faced image of perfect femininity is printed in society periodicals, such as *Life* and *Harper's*.

### THERMIONIC DIODE VALVE
British electrical engineer John Ambrose Fleming patents the thermionic diode (two electrode) valve (vacuum tube). It allows current to pass in one direction only and will be used for years as a key component in radio and T.V. receivers. After 1947, it will be gradually replaced by transistors.

### TEA IN A BAG
Tea bags are unwittingly introduced by Thomas Sullivan, a New York wholesaler who sends samples of tea to his customers in small silk bags instead of tins.

# RUSSIAN UPRISING AND RELATIVITY

Revolution breaks out in Russia when czarist troops fire on demonstrators outside the Winter Palace in St. Petersburg. A mutiny follows and the czar is forced to introduce reform. After bitter fighting, the Russo-Japanese War comes to an end, with Japan victorious. Norway declares independence from Sweden and Albert Einstein publishes his theory of relativity.

## 1905

| | | |
|---|---|---|
| **Jan** | **2** | Russia surrenders Port Arthur to Japan |
| | **22** | Czar's troops massacre peaceful demonstrators in St. Petersburg |
| **Mar** | **24** | French writer Jules Verne (b.1828) dies |
| **May** | **27** | Battle of Tsu Shima. Japanese devastate Russian Baltic fleet |
| **June** | **7** | *Die Brücke* exhibition in Dresden |
| | **27** | Mutiny on the battleship *Potemkin* |

| | | |
|---|---|---|
| **Aug** | **19** | Duma, a representative assembly, is established in Russia |
| **Sep** | **5** | Russia and Japan sign peace treaty to end Russo-Japanese War |
| **Oct** | **1** | The Fauves exhibit in Paris |
| | **14** | English suffragettes Christobel Pankhurst and Annie Kenney are imprisoned |
| | **26** | Norway separates from Sweden |
| **Nov** | **28** | Universal suffrage in Austria |

BELOW: Cars for millionaires.  A 4 cylinder Fiat is on display.

# RUSSIA ARISES

In January, strikers marching through the Russian capital of St. Petersburg to petition Czar Nicholas II for better conditions are shot dead by troops defending the Winter Palace. More than 500 are killed and many more wounded. The massacre increases demands for reform in Russia.

In June, Russian sailors on the battleship *Potemkin* mutiny after complaints about conditions on board. Other ships in the port of Odessa join the mutiny, while the city is gripped by a general strike. The mutiny adds to the weakening of the czar's rule.

In October, Czar Nicholas II agrees to a new constitution and turns Russia from an absolute autocracy into a semi-constitutional monarchy. The change is forced on him by a general strike which has paralyzed the country for months, as well as the defeat in the war against Japan.

BELOW: *Potemkin* mutiny. A burnt-out railway shed is left devastated after mutineers rampage through Odessa.

RIGHT: Battleship *Potemkin*, where the shooting of a sailor sparks off a serious mutiny.

### THE KAISER IN AFRICA

The visit of the German Kaiser Wilhelm II (1859–1941) to Morocco leads to tension between Germany and France, who have traditionally claimed "a special standing" in Morocco. The Kaiser claims he is protecting German economic interests.

### SALOME AND THE SEVEN VEILS

Based on Oscar Wilde's scandalous 1893 play, Richard Strauss's opera *Salome* opens in Dresden. Its striking harmonies and large orchestra (requiring singers of great power) establish Strauss (1864–1949) as the major German opera composer of the time. The famous Dance of the Seven Veils causes a scandal.

### FREE NORWAY

The Norwegian parliament in Oslo declares independence from Sweden in June. The result is approved by the people in a plebiscite in August and Norway becomes an independent nation in October. Prince Charles of Denmark accepts the throne and rules as Haakon VII (1872–1957).

### EINSTEIN, RELATIVITY, AND OTHER THEORIES

German-born physicist Albert Einstein (1879–1955) publishes his Special Theory of Relativity, in which he revolutionizes thinking by proposing that time and motion are relative. He also publishes papers on Brownian motion and the photoelectric effect.

### SOCIOLOGY RECOGNIZED

The American Sociological Society is formed in Chicago, Illinois, marking sociology's acceptance by the academic world. It follows the founding by the University of Chicago of the world's first sociology department, headed by Albion Small, and the publication of the first sociology journal.

### DIE BRUCKE EXPRESS THEMSELVES

A group of German artists in Dresden mount their first exhibition in a lamp factory. They are the first Expressionists. The founding members are Fritz Bleyl, Erich Heckel, Ludwig Kirchner, and Karl Schmidt-Rottluff (who gave the group its name, *Die Brücke*, meaning the bridge). Their bold outlines and strong planes of color enliven European art for several years and have a lasting influence.

### SPEED WARNINGS

The Automobile Association is founded in Britain to warn car drivers of police speed traps. The speed limit is 20 mph.

### RADIOTHORIUM

German radio chemist Otto Hahn (1879–1968) discovers radiothorium, a radioactive isotope produced by the breakdown and decay of the radioactive chemical element thorium.

### EARLY STRUGGLE FOR CIVIL RIGHTS

The militant Niagara Movement is founded in the United States by 29 black intellectuals from 14 states, led by Atlanta University professor William Edward Burghardt Du Bois. They demand universal male suffrage and the abolition of discrimination based on race or color.

### WILD BEASTS IN PARIS

Work by the artists Matisse, Marquet, Derain, Vlaminck, Rouault and others is hung in the same room at the Salon d'Automne. The mass effect of bright color and distorted patterns earns them the nickname Les Fauves (the wild beasts).

BELOW: Hussars charge striking workers in Warsaw.

## MAGNETIC NORTH TRACKED DOWN
Norwegian explorer Roald Amundsen (1872–1928) completes the passage from the Pacific to the Atlantic along the Arctic coast. On the way, he finds the current position of magnetic north.

## NORDIC GAMES
The Scandinavian nations compete in the first Nordic Games. The event, which features cross-country skiing and ski jumping, is later overshadowed by the Winter Olympics.

## FIRST SUFFRAGETTES IN PRISON
In the U.K., Christabel Pankhurst (1880–1958) and Annie Kenney, of the militant women's suffrage movement, choose prison rather than fines. They have been convicted of assaulting policemen after having been forcibly ejected from a political meeting for demanding votes for women.

## SILK FOR EVERYONE
Rayon, a new fabric dubbed "artificial silk," is to be produced by the British textile company, Courtaulds. They have bought the U.K. manufacturing rights from its British inventor, C.H. Stearn, who patented it in 1898. It is used for underwear and stockings.

## WASSERMAN TEST
German bacteriologist August Wasserman (1866–1925) develops a test for the disease syphilis.

## PIZZA TO GO
The United States' first pizzeria, Lombardi's on Spring Street in Little Italy, New York City, begins to sell pizza, a Neapolitan dish. It proves a popular fast food with busy New Yorkers.

## TENNIS ANYONE?
May Sutton becomes the first American to win a title at the Wimbledon Tennis Tournament. She becomes the Ladies' Singles Champion.

## TESTING FOR CHILDREN
Alfred Binet (1857–1911), director of the Psychological Laboratory at the Sorbonne in Paris, and his colleague, Theodore Simon, produce tests to classify children according to their mental ability. This is in response to the French government's request in 1904 for them to study children with special educational needs.

## SPECIAL NEEDS PIONEERS
The first special needs schools for educationally disadvantaged children are introduced in the Netherlands and subsidized by the state.

RIGHT: New York's elevated railway.

ABOVE: President Roosevelt watches submarine *Plunger* go through its paces.

# EARTHQUAKES AND CORNFLAKES

Cubism is born with the work of Pablo Picasso, who introduces a revolutionary new way of painting the human form. In architecture, Antonio Gaudí breaks with tradition by introducing startling new designs to the city of Barcelona. The eruption of Mt. Vesuvius in Italy and a major earthquake in San Francisco cause immense suffering and destruction.

OPPOSITE: Wreckage after Russian revolutionaries bomb Premier Stolypin's home.

## 1906

| | | |
|---|---|---|
| **Feb** | 10 | HMS *Dreadnought* is launched |
| **Apr** | 7 | Mt. Vesuvius erupts in Italy |
| | 8 | Treaty of Algeciras ends Moroccan crisis |
| | 18 | San Francisco is devastated by an earthquake |
| **May** | 10 | First Duma meets in Russia |
| | 23 | Norwegian dramatist Henrik Ibsen dies |
| **June** | 26 | World's first Grand Prix is held in Le Mans, France |
| **July** | 12 | Alfred Dreyfus is awarded the Legion of Honor |
| **Oct** | 22 | Paul Cézanne dies |
| | 23 | Suffragettes imprisoned after a demonstration at the Houses of Parliament in the U.K. |

ABOVE: Christian Science temple, Boston, founded by Mary Baker Eddy.

ABOVE: King Alfonso of Spain and his new bride Victoria travel in state through Madrid, minutes before an anarchist hurls a bomb.

## MOROCCAN CRISIS

France, Spain, Britain, and Germany meet for a conference in Algeciras, Spain, to decide the future of Morocco. The four powers agree to the continuing independence of Morocco under the Sultan of Morocco, but with Spain and France jointly policing the country. The treaty strengthens the Anglo-French Entente Cordiale and further isolates Germany.

## FIRST GRAND PRIX

The world's first Grand Prix motor race takes place in France. The 65 mile event lasts two days and is won by Hungarian driver Ferenc Szisz, who averages a speed of 62 mph.

## HOT DOG

Hot dogs become fast food after "Tad" Dorgan, a Chicago cartoonist, draws a dachshund inside a Frankfurter bun.

## DREYFUS NOT GUILTY

After eleven years, the French government formally annuls the guilty verdict given to Alfred Dreyfus, a Jew and a military officer wrongly accused of treason and spying against France. He is awarded the Legion of Honor. The case has split France and revealed considerable anti-Semitism in the country.

## MAGNETIC POLE

Norwegian explorer Roald Amundsen (1872–1928) reaches the Pacific Ocean in the *Gjöa*, after a three year voyage. During this journey, he plotted the North Magnetic Pole and discovered the Northwest Passage, the sea route from the Atlantic Ocean through the Arctic archipelago.

## BARCELONA TRANSFORMED

Catalan architect Antonio Gaudí (1852–1926) has designed a house, Casa Battló, for a Barcelona textile manufacturer. Its curving walls, roof like a lizard's back, use of tiles and colored glazing are all distinctive features of Gaudí's style as he emerges from Art Nouveau. After Gaudí, Barcelona never looks the same again.

LEFT: Eighteen bystanders are killed and the state carriage wrecked by the bomb; King Alfonso and Queen Victoria survive.

BELOW: Balloonists prepare to break the long distance flight record.

## VOTES FOR WOMEN

Women in Finland become the first women in Europe to gain the vote. The following year, 19 women have seats in Finland's parliament. By contrast, in the U.K., women's fight for the vote becomes increasingly militant as women throughout the country heckle political meetings in the lead-up to the general election. In June, a deputation representing some half a million women march on the Houses of Parliament to present a petition to the new Liberal government, demanding votes for women. Its rejection is followed by a huge rally in London's Trafalgar Square. In October, women disrupt the state opening of Parliament and ten members of the WSPU are imprisoned rather than pay fines. This year, the militant tactics of WSPU members gain them the nickname "suffragettes," following an insult in the *Daily Mail* newspaper.

## IBERIA

Spanish composer Isaac Albéniz begins the suite for piano that will become his most famous work. Inspired by the music and dance rhythms of Andalusia, Iberia shows Spanish composers how they can express national character in music.

## SIMPLON TUNNEL

One of Europe's longest rail tunnels, the Simplon Tunnel connecting Brig in Switzerland with Iselle in Italy, is opened. It is about 12 miles long.

## CUBISM IS BORN

Pablo Picasso (1881–1973) produces *Les Demoiselles d'Avignon*, the pivotal painting of the early twentieth century. Its angular handling of human forms is so shocking that he is very selective about who sees the picture. From this painting derives Cubism and all the other art movements in which natural subjects are broken up into a new synthesis of form.

## ELECTRIC WASHING MACHINE

American Alva J. Fisher patents the first electric washing machine, marking the beginning of a major reduction in household drudgery.

BELOW: City Hall is in ruins after an earthquake and three day firestorm devastate San Francisco. Above, a policeman stands in the wreckage.

## BREAKFAST CEREAL

Will Keith Kellogg and his partner Charles D. Bolin incorporate the Battle Creek Toasted Corn Flake Co. to sell their breakfast cereals. Their new Sanitas cornflakes are lighter and crisper than their first cornflakes, produced in 1898.

## NATURAL DISASTERS

Mt. Vesuvius erupts in April destroying the town of Ottaiano and causing damage in nearby Naples. In the United States that same month, a severe earthquake hits San Francisco. The tremors and the following three day firestorm almost destroy the city.

## HMS DREADNOUGHT

Britain launches the battleship HMS *Dreadnought*, the fastest and most heavily armored warship yet built. As an "all big gun" ship, *Dreadnought* also carries the heaviest firepower with ten 12 inch guns.

---

### PAUL CEZANNE
### (1839–1906)

Paul Cézanne, the French painter, has died. His work increasingly concentrated on the underlying forms of nature. It was not widely recognized until the last ten years of his life but will widely influence the development of abstract art. His best-known paintings include *The Card Players* (1890–1892), *Aix: Paysage Rocheux* (1887) and *The Gardener* (1906).

---

# GANDHI, BALLOONS, AND HELICOPTERS

Norwegian women gain the vote, following their Finnish sisters the previous year. Transport makes strides as the world's first "helicopter" makes a successful flight. The liner *Lusitania* crosses the Atlantic at record speed and French balloonists make the first-ever aerial crossing of the North Sea. Gandhi introduces the idea of nonviolent civil disobedience. Home laundry becomes easier with new washing machines and washing powder.

OPPOSITE: The great nebula of Orion photographed at Yerkes Observatory, near Chicago.

## 1 9 0 7

| | | |
|---|---|---|
| Jan | 14 | Earthquake hits Jamaica |
| Mar | 22 | Gandhi begins a civil disobedience campaign in South Africa |
| June | 14 | Norwegian women gain the right to vote |
| | 16 | Duma dissolved in Russia |
| July | 29 | Boy Scouts are founded in the U.K. |
| Aug | 4 | French fleet bombard Casablanca after antiforeign riots |
| Sep | 26 | New Zealand becomes a dominion of Great Britain |
| Nov | 13 | Cornu makes the first helicopter flight in France |
| Dec | 10 | Rudyard Kipling wins the Nobel Prize for literature |

ABOVE: Paris rubbish is discharged through huge pipes to be treated and converted into electricity.

## CIVIL DISOBEDIENCE

In South Africa, Mohandâs Gandhi (1869–1948) begins a campaign of civil disobedience, or *satyagraha*, against the state government in protest to its new law that requires all Indians to register their presence, submit to being fingerprinted, and carry a certificate of registration with them at all times. Gandhi declares that the new law discriminates against the Indian population in the Transvaal.

## DISSOLUTION OF DUMA

In St Petersburg, the Russian Czar Nicholas II (1868–1918) dissolves the Duma, or parliament, when his prime minister, Peter Stolypin, accuses 55 socialist deputies of plotting against the czar. The czar had hoped that the Duma would contain deputies favorable to his conservative policies. Instead, it contains liberals and socialists intent on radical reform.

## NORWEGIAN WOMEN GAIN THE VOTE

The Norwegian parliament agrees to allow women to vote in elections on the same terms as men. It follows the decision of the Finnish parliament to grant women the vote last year, but since Finland is a province of Russia, Norway is the first independent European country to grant universal suffrage.

## MOTHER

Russian novelist Maxim Gorky (1868–1936) publishes *Mother*, an influential novel about revolutionaries.

## SUFFRAGETTES BATTLE WITH POLICE

In the U.K., suffragettes demonstrate outside and storm the House of Commons. Their actions are met by considerable police brutality. Increasing numbers of women are imprisoned.

## TRIPLE ALLIANCE RENEWED

Germany, Austria, and Italy renew the Triple Alliance between their three countries for another six years, despite Italian reservations. The alliance faces increasingly close links between France and Britain. The following month, Britain signs an understanding with Russia, which draws Russia into their alliance.

## NEW ZEALAND

After 48 years as a British colony, New Zealand becomes an independent dominion in the British Empire, joining Australia and Canada.

## DYING SWAN

Russian ballerina Anna Pavlova (1885–1931) dances the Dying Swan in *Swan Lake*. Choreographed by Mikhail Fokine, the dance becomes Pavlova's trademark. She will dance it, to Saint-Saëns' music, with the Ballets Russes in Paris, and later with her own company. It becomes an icon of classical ballet.

## HENRI MATISSE

The painting *Blue Nude* by French artist Henri Matisse (1869–1954) causes offense to more conservative viewers. The artist painted it after a short visit to North Africa and combined a classical pose with a primitive treatment. It is the primitivism that distinguishes Matisse and which has also caused offense.

BELOW: Damming the waters of the Nile threatens the Temple of Isis on the island of Philae.

ABOVE: World leaders meet for a peace conference at The Hague. They discuss methods of resolving conflict.

## RIOTS IN MOROCCO
The French fleet bombards the port of Casablanca and French troops occupy the city after Moroccans riot against foreign workers. More than 1,000 Moors are killed.

## BOY SCOUTS FOUNDED
In the U.K., Boer War veteran Sir Robert Baden-Powell sets up a new organization for boys based on his army experience. The organization is known as the "boy scouts."

## PLAYBOY CAUSES RIOTS
Riots follow the premiere of playwright John Synge's *The Playboy of the Western World*. Performed at the Abbey Theatre, the play's portrayal of Irish life is too realistic for the audience. There are more riots as the play goes on tour, but it will ultimately be recognized as an Irish classic.

## THE PRAYER
Constantin Brancusi (1876–1957), the Romanian sculptor, leads the way towards abstract sculpture with his work *The Prayer*. A funeral monument, the statue shows a young girl kneeling in prayer. Its simplified form will herald the development of abstract painting.

## FIRST VERTICAL TAKEOFF
French bicycle dealer and inventor Pierre Cornu makes the world's first free flight by "helicopter." Cornu's machine has twin motor-driven rotors and a 24 horsepower engine and lifts vertically off the ground.

## LUSITANIA IS THE WORLD'S FASTEST LINER
The Cunard liner *Lusitania*, built in 1906, captures the Blue Riband of the Atlantic, a national trophy for the fastest crossing. She makes the crossing from Liverpool to New York at an average speed of 23.99 knots.

## MOTORCYCLE RACING
Motorcycle enthusiasts set up a racing festival on the Isle of Man, off the British coast, after racing is banned on mainland roads.

ABOVE: Irish suffragist Miss Maloney rings a handbell, successfully bringing to an end a speech by Liberal candidate Mr. Winston Churchill, noted opponent of votes for women.

## "JEWISH MARK TWAIN"

Author Sholem Aleichem has begun to publish his series of stories, *Mottel, or The Cantor's Son*. Written in Yiddish (later translated into English), they give expression to the experiences and humor of ordinary Jewish people in the United States. Publication continues until 1916 and Aleichem becomes known as the "Jewish Mark Twain."

## A BETTER VALVE

American inventor Lee de Forest improves the diode valve invented by J.A. Fleming in 1904, by introducing a third electrode. This creates a triode valve. The third electrode, called a grid, has holes in it. By varying the electric charge on the grid, the flow of electrons can be varied.

## CAUSE OF SCURVY

The British biochemist Frederick Gowland Hopkins suggests that lack of certain trace substances in the diet can cause diseases such as rickets and scurvy. The substances are later named vitamins.

## SUICIDE COUNSELLING

A suicide counselling service is opened in New York City by the Salvation Army.

## OVER THE NORTH SEA

The first aerial crossing of the North Sea is made in the balloon *Mammoth* in October by three French aeronauts. The flight is from Crystal Palace, London, to the shores of Lake Vänern, Sweden, a distance of about 725 miles.

## ELEMENT DISCOVERED

The French chemist Georges Urbain discovers the heaviest of the rare-earth elements, lutetium. A radioactive isotope of the element becomes useful in determining the age of meteorites.

## ITALIAN WINS RACE

Entering the French capital two months ahead of the nearest competitor, Prince Scipione Borghese of Italy wins the Peking-to-Paris Automobile Race by a huge margin. Borghese and his mechanic covered 9,317 miles in 62 days.

## NATURAL DISASTERS

In January, a massive earthquake flattens Jamaica. Just one week later, a tidal wave sweeps the Dutch East Indies.

## NURSING HONOR

Florence Nightingale, now aged 87, blind, and an invalid, becomes the first woman to be awarded the British Order of Merit. The honor is conferred by King Edward VII for her services to the nursing profession.

LEFT: Hundreds of acres of tobacco are grown under cheesecloth in Puerto Rico. It is an American invention for increasing yield.

BELOW: The Cresta Run in Switzerland. It is the world's most famous toboggan run.

## RECORD IMMIGRATION
1907 is a record year for immigration to the U.S., with more than one million people granted citizenship.

## NEW WASHING POWDER
Persil, a washing powder produced by Henkel & Cie in Düsseldorf, Germany, is marketed in Britain for washing clothes.

## AGITATED WASHING MACHINE
Thor, the first electric agitator washing machine, is marketed by the Hurley Machine Company in the States. It was designed by U.S. engineer John Hurley, who has used an electric motor to power a rotating dolly.

## NEW ZOO
In Hamburg, Carl Hagenbeck creates a new kind of zoo. Animals live freely in their natural habitats.

### DMITRI IVANOVICH MENDELEYEV
### (1834–1907)

The Russian scientist Dmitri Mendeleyev dies this year. His work on the grouping of elements according to their atomic weight accurately predicted the properties of several elements that were waiting to be discovered. He also studied the aeronautics and behavior of gases and, in 1887, took a pioneering ascent in an air balloon.

# CARS FOR EVERYBODY

A two year old child becomes the last Manchu emperor of China. The first modern version of the Olympic Games is held and the first vacuum cleaner goes on sale in the United States. The largest earthquake ever recorded in Europe devastates the Italian town of Messina and the dream of motoring for the masses becomes a reality when the American car manufacturer, Henry Ford, begins production of the new Model T motor car.

OPPOSITE: French can-can dancers wow audiences at London nightclubs.

## 1908

| | | |
|---|---|---|
| Feb | 1 | King Carlos and Prince Luiz of Portugal are assassinated |
| June | 21 | 200,000 attend a suffragette rally in the U.K. |
| July | 13 | Olympic Games begin in the U.K. |
| Aug | 12 | Henry Ford's first assembly line Model T appears |
| | 19 | Congo, Africa becomes a Belgian colony |
| Oct | 5 | Bulgaria declared independent |
| | 6 | Austria annexes Bosnia and Herzegovina |
| Nov | 14 | Chinese Dowager Empress dies |
| Dec | 2 | Three year old Pu Yi becomes Emperor of China |
| | 28 | Earthquake devastates Messina, Sicily |

ABOVE: Giant bamboo growing in the Botanical Gardens at Peradeniya, Ceylon. In the countryside, these densely packed trees are vulnerable to fire.

ABOVE: Orville Wright prepares for his flight.

### BELGIAN CONGO
Leopold II, king of Belgium, hands over his vast private estate in central Africa to the control of the Belgian government. Belgium thus acquires its first colony, which is more than 90 times its own size.

### EARTHQUAKE DEVASTATION
A massive earthquake, the biggest ever recorded in Europe, destroys the town of Messina in Sicily, southern Italy. Thousands of people are killed and made homeless.

### THE BALKANS
In the Balkans, King Ferdinand I (1861–1948) declares Bulgaria independent from Turkey and takes the title of czar. At the same time, Austria annexes the Turkish province of Bosnia-Herzegovina and Crete proclaims its union with Greece. The Ottoman Empire continues to disintegrate.

### MAKING AMMONIA
German chemist Fritz Haber (1868–1934) invents the Haber process for making ammonia artificially by combining nitrogen and hydrogen.

ABOVE: Orville Wright swoops over Fort Myer, Virginia. An accident during this military air trial kills Wright's companion, T.E. Selfridge.

### CHILD EMPEROR
After the deaths of the Emperor Kuang Hsu and the Dowager Empress Tsu-Hsi, the three year old Pu Yi becomes emperor of China with the name Emperor Hsuan T'ung. Real power lies with the various warlords who control the Chinese throne.

### MASS PRODUCED MODEL T
American car manufacturer Henry Ford (1863–1947) begins the mass production of his Model T Ford car, using an innovative assembly line method. He sells the new model for $850, but by 1925 has cut the price to $260. When production stops in 1927 he has made 15 million Model Ts.

### THE WAR IN THE AIR
In this prophetic novel, H.G. Wells describes the military use of aircraft, a form of warfare which will soon become all too well-known. This prediction later helps to give Wells the status of modern prophet.

## POWER AT LAST
After earlier failures, American inventor Thomas Alva Edison (1847–1931) perfects his alkaline storage battery. It stores more than twice as much power as a lead-acid battery.

## DETECTING RADIATION
While working in Manchester, England, German physicist Hans Geiger (1882–1945) invents the Geiger counter, a device which detects radiation. It works by detecting and counting alpha particles emitted by a radioactive substance.

## "THE EIGHT"
A group of American painters who have had work rejected from the National Academy of Design form "the Eight," part of what will later become known as the Ashcan School. They are ridiculed as "apostles of ugliness" and exhibit together only once.

## MAGNETIC SUNSPOTS
American astronomer George Ellery Hale (1868–1938) discovers that sunspots have strong magnetic fields. They are the first magnetic fields detected outside the Earth. He also installs a 59 inch reflecting telescope at Mount Wilson Observatory in California.

## SPACE–TIME LINK-UP
Professor Hermann Minkowski, a Lithuanian mathematician, puts forward the view that space and time are interlinked as the "space-time continuum."

## CELLOPHANE
Swiss chemist Dr. Jacques Edwin Brandenburger patents a thin, transparent, flexible film made from wood cellulose. He calls it Cellophane.

## EXPEDITION TO ANTARCTIC
Ernest Shackleton and Edward Wilson, with the National Antarctic Expedition, travel to latitude 88° 22' S, closer to the South Pole than any previous expeditions.

## LIQUID HELIUM
Dutch physicist Heike Kamerlingh Onnes (1853–1926) discovers how to make the gas helium into a liquid. This strange liquid expands instead of contracting as it cools and conducts heat well.

## INTERNATIONAL PSYCHOLOGY CONGRESS
The first International Congress of Psychology is held in Salzburg in April. It is attended by the leading figures in this controversial new branch of medicine, including Sigmund Freud and his colleagues Alfred Adler and Karl Jung.

## A NEW CHAMPION
Texan Jack Johnson becomes the first black heavyweight boxing champion of the world.

## FIRST PSYCHOLOGY TEXTBOOK
The first social psychology textbook is published by William McDougall, a British psychologist who argues for a biological rather than a philosophical approach to psychology. He believes people inherit instincts and characteristics that direct them to unconscious goals.

## MARATHON RUNNER DISQUALIFIED
London, England, steps in to host the Fourth Olympic Games after Rome, Italy withdraws. Large crowds watch as the games are held as a self-contained event. The marathon ends in drama when Italian runner Dorando Pietri is helped across the finish line in first place. He is stripped of his gold medal as the help is against the rules, but wins public sympathy.

## DISPOSABLE CUPS
Disposable paper cups are introduced into the States by the International Paper Company, a conglomerate of American and Canadian paper companies.

## CHAMPAGNE DISASTER
In Champagne, France, the last European wine region to be devastated by the vine-destroying phylloxera aphid has its worst harvest failure this century. The year's total production equals little more than that normally produced by one vineyard.

## VACUUM CLEANER
The first commercial vacuum cleaner is produced in the States by William Hoover, a leather manufacturer.

ABOVE: Residues of pitchblende are stirred in these tanks to produce radioactive radium, first discovered by Pierre and Marie Curie.

# BLERIOT AND BALLETS RUSSES

Louis Blériot makes headlines when he successfully flies across the English Channel. He is the first man to do so. The Ballets Russes is formed and brings dramatic innovation to the world of ballet. In Berlin, the AEG Turbine Factory proves that modern architecture can blend perfectly with the demands of industry. The world's first synthetic plastic is invented and the first newsreels appear in cinemas. Neon lights shine in the night. In Holland, the first organized 11 city ice skating tour takes place. In Britain, imprisoned suffragettes go on a hunger strike.

## 1909

| | | |
|---|---|---|
| Jan | 1 | Old age pensions are introduced in the U.K. |
| Mar | 31 | Pathé News shown in Paris |
| Apr | 6 | Robert Peary reaches the North Pole |
| | 23 | Armenians are massacred in Turkey |
| | 27 | Young Turks depose Sultan Abdul Hamid |
| May | 18 | Ballets Russes performs in Paris |
| July | 16 | Twelve year old Soltan Ahmed Mirza becomes the Shah of Persia |
| | 25 | Blériot flies the Channel |
| Oct | 26 | Japan's first prime minister, Prince Ito Hirobumi, is assassinated |
| Dec | 16 | President Jose Zelaya resigns in Nicaragua |

ABOVE: Royal England meets Imperial Russia. Pictured are the Prince of Wales and the Czar with their sons.

ABOVE: Polar base camp. From here, on April 6, American commander Robert Peary is the first man to reach the North Pole..

## ARMENIAN MASSACRES
Thousands of Armenians are killed by Turks in the province of Cilicia in April. Sultan Abdul-Hamid (1842–1918) orders the killings after Armenian revolutionaries, demonstrating against oppressive Turkish rule, provoke the inhabitants and officials in Armenia. The United States and various European countries intervene to halt the killings. Following these events, Abdul Hamid is deposed by a unanimous vote in the two houses of parliament that he was forced to set up the previous year. Opposition to the sultan is led by the Young Turks, who are pressing for reform in the vast and ramshackle Ottoman Empire. The sultan is replaced by his brother, Mahmud Reshad.

## BLERIOT FLIES THE CHANNEL
The first man to fly across the English Channel is Louis Blériot (1872–1936) of France, flying a monoplane he has designed and built himself. His historic flight, from Calais to Dover, takes just 37 minutes.

## MOROCCO
French and Spanish forces fight Rif tribesmen in Morocco as the Moroccan War continues.

## NICARAGUAN CIVIL WAR
War begins in Nicaragua with a conservative revolt against liberal dictator President Jose Santos Zelaya. Dr. Jose Madriz is elected to succeed him.

## BALLETS RUSSES FOUNDED
Russian impresario Sergei Diaghilev (1872–1929) founds the company that will have the greatest influence over ballet in the twentieth century. Many of his dancers, choreographers, and artists are Russian exiles, including Nijinsky, Pavlova, Karsavina, Fokine, and Stravinsky. He also draws on the best of French talent. The company is notable for its new fusion of passion, fantasy, color, and sound with classical ballet.

## HUNGER STRIKES
In the U.K., imprisoned suffragettes begin to go on a hunger strike. The British government orders them to be forcibly fed and there is a public outcry.

## GLASGOW SCHOOL OF ART
Charles Rennie Macintosh brings Art Nouveau and Viennese Secession styles to Scotland in his own unique idiom. This building is one of the finest examples. It is famous because of its innovative use of space, unusual ornament, and inspired use of vertical elements. The library is finished in 1909 and is the best of all.

## INDUSTRY MEETS ARCHITECTURE
Designed by pioneering German architect Peter Behrens (1868–1940), the AEG Turbine Factory in Berlin shows for the first time that the modern architectural idiom is well-suited to industrial buildings. It demonstrates that such buildings can, in themselves, be fine examples of architecture. Huge windows provide lots of light and metal uprights and roofing beams give a broad roof span. No ornament is used, but the structure itself has an austere elegance.

## BAKELITE IS THE FIRST SYNTHETIC PLASTIC

A Belgian-born American industrial chemist, Leo Hendrik Baekeland, markets the world's first heatproof synthetic plastic. It is called phenolic resin but is better known under its trade name, Bakelite. It proves to be an excellent electrical insulator.

## FIRST CINEMA NEWSREEL

French film pioneer Charles Pathé (1863–1957) begins making and showing the first cinema newsreel in Paris. He takes the idea to the United States in 1910.

## DARING TO BE GAY

His novel, *Strait is the Gate*, launches Parisian writer André Gide (1869–1951) on a courageous career as a novelist. He defends his own right to be gay, but in this book pays tribute to his wife who appears as the character Madeleine.

## LIGHTING UP WITH NEON

French scientist Georges Claude invents the neon tube, in which a glass tube containing a small quantity of neon gas glows red when a current is passed through it. Different colors are produced by adding other gases.

## AUTOMATIC TOAST

The first electric toaster is sold in America by the General Electric Company. It toasts the bread on only one side at a time and doesn't eject the toast.

## PENSIONS FOR THE ELDERLY

In Britain, old-age pensions are introduced for people aged 70 and over. France introduced old-age insurance in 1850, followed by Germany, Denmark, and New Zealand. Britain's is the first twentieth century scheme and is the most comprehensive to date.

ABOVE: Louis Blériot stands in his monoplane before takeoff. Later that day he becomes the first man to fly the Channel, flying from France to England in just 37 minutes.

ABOVE: Following his inauguration, President Taft and his wife ride to the White House. He succeeds former president Roosevelt.

## RADIO SEA RESCUE

The first use of radio to save life at sea is made when the ship *Republic* collides with another vessel in the Atlantic and calls for help. The rescuers arrive in time to save nearly all the passengers.

## SIX PIECES FOR LARGE ORCHESTRA

This pivotal work of the Second Viennese School, composed by Anton Webern, is notable for its use of wind and percussion instruments to produce a unique orchestral color and sense of space.

## PEARL HARBOR SELECTED

President Taft announces that Pearl Harbor has been chosen as the the site for the Navy's principal base in the Pacific.

## TAKE STOCK IN AMERICA

Private citizens owning stock in America's biggest corporations now total over two million and are estimated to be earning over $1 billion a year in dividends.

## LILIOM: PLAY, MUSICAL, AND FILM

Hungarian writer Ferenc Molnár publishes *Liliom*, his most famous play. Subsequently it is turned first into a musical (1945) and then the film *Carousel* (1956).

## PEARY REACHES THE NORTH POLE

Robert E. Peary, a U.S. naval commander, is the first person to reach the North Pole. This is his second attempt. He is accompanied during the final stages by his colleague, Matthew Henson, and four Inuit.

## A NEW WORD

The National Conservation Commission, appointed by President Roosevelt, publishes the first inventory of the United States' natural resources. Advised by his chief forester, Gifford Pinchot, who has coined the term "conservation." Roosevelt has already introduced several legislative measures designed to preserve the natural environment.

### GERONIMO
### (1829–1909)

The Apache leader Geronimo, who led the Apache Indians in their struggle against Mexican, and later North American usurpers, has died. After finally surrendering in 1886, he became a Christian and farmed in Oklahoma. His Native American name was Goyathlay which translates as "one who yawns."

# WINNERS AND ACHIEVERS OF THE 1900s

## NOBEL PRIZES

The Nobel Prizes are an international award granted in the fields of literature, physics, chemistry, physiology or medicine, and peace. The first prizes were awarded in 1901 and funded by the money left in the will of the Swedish inventor, Alfred Nobel (1833–1896), who gave the world dynamite.

### PRIZES FOR LITERATURE

**1901** Rene Sully-Prudhomme (French) for poetry
**1902** Theodor Mommsen (German) for historical narratives
**1903** Bjornstjerne Bjornson (Norwegian) for fiction, poetry and drama
**1904** Frederic Mistral (French) for poetry, and Jose Echegaray y Eizaguirre (Spanish) for drama
**1905** Henryk Sienkiewicz (Polish) for fiction
**1906** Giosue Carducci (Italian) for poetry
**1907** Rudyard Kipling (British) for fiction and poetry
**1908** Rudolf Eucken (German) for philosophic writings
**1909** Selma Lagerlof (Swedish) for fiction and poetry

### PRIZES FOR PEACE

**1901** Jean Henri Dunant (Swiss) for founding the Red Cross and originating the Geneva Convention, and Frederic Passy (French) for founding a French peace society
**1902** Elie Ducommun (Swiss) for work as honorary secretary of the International Peace Bureau, and Charles Albert Gobat (Swiss) for administrating the Inter-Parliamentary Union
**1903** Sir William Cremer (British) for activities as founder and secretary of the International Arbitration League
**1904** The Institute of International Law for studies on the laws of neutrality and other phases of international law
**1905** Baroness Bertha von Suttner (Austrian) for promoting pacifism and founding an Austrian peace society
**1906** Theodore Roosevelt (American) for negotiating peace in the Russo-Japanese War
**1907** Ernesto Moneta (Italian) for work as president of the Lombard League for Peace, and Louis Renault (French) for work on peace conferences

**1908** Klas Pontus Arnoldson (Swedish) for founding the Swedish Society for Arbitration and Peace, and Fredrik Bajer (Danish) for work on the International Peace Bureau
**1909** Auguste Beernaert (Belgian) for work on the Permanent Court of Arbitration, and Paul d'Estournelles (French) for founding and directing the French Parliamentary Arbitration Committee and League of International Conciliation

### PRIZES FOR PHYSICS

**1901** Wilhelm Roentgen (German) for discovering X-rays
**1902** Hendrik Antoon Lorentz and Pieter Zeeman (Dutch) for noting the Zeeman effect of magnetism on light
**1903** Antoine Henri Becquerel and Pierre and Marie Curie (French) for discovering radioactivity and studying uranium
**1904** Baron Rayleigh (British) for studying the density of gases and discovering argon
**1905** Philipp Lenard (German) for studying the properties of cathode rays.
**1906** Sir Joseph John Thomson (British) for studying electrical discharge through gases.
**1907** Albert Michelson (American) for the design of precise optical instruments and for accurate measurements.
**1908** Gabriel Lippman (French) for his method of color photography.
**1909** Guglielmo Marconi (Italian) and Karl Ferdinand Braun (German) for developing the wireless telegraph

### PRIZES FOR CHEMISTRY

**1901** Jacobus Henricus Van't Hoff (Dutch) for discovering laws of chemical dynamics and osmotic pressure
**1902** Emil Fischer (German) for synthesizing sugars, purine derivatives and peptides
**1903** Svante August Arrhenius (Swedish) for the dissociation theory of ionization in electrolytes
**1904** Sir William Ramsay (British) for discovering helium, neon, xenon and krypton and determining their place in the periodic system

**1905** Adolf von Baeyer (German) for work on dyes and organic compounds and for synthesizing indigo and arsenicals
**1906** Henri Moissan (French) for preparing pure fluorine and developing the electric furnace
**1907** Eduard Buchner (German) for biochemical researches and for discovering cell-less fermentation
**1908** Ernest Rutherford (British) for discovering that radioactive elements change into other elements
**1909** Wilhelm Ostwald (German) for work on catalysis, chemical equilibrium and the rate of chemical reactions

### PRIZES FOR PHYSIOLOGY OR MEDICINE

**1901** Emil von Behring (German) for discovering the diphtheria antitoxin
**1902** Sir Ronald Ross (British) for discovering how malaria is transmitted
**1903** Niels Ryberg Finsen (Danish) for treating diseases, especially lupus vulgaris, with concentrated light rays
**1904** Ivan Petrovich Pavlov (Russian) for work on the physiology of digestion.
**1905** Robert Koch (German) for working on tuberculosis and discovering the tubercle bacillus and tuberculin
**1906** Camillo Golgi (Italian) and Santiago Ramon y Cajal (Spanish) for studies of nerve tissue
**1907** Charles Louis Alphonse Laveran (French) for studying diseases caused by protozoans
**1908** Paul Ehrlich (German) and Elie Metchnikoff (Russian) for work on immunity
**1909** Emil Theodor Kocher (Swiss) for work on the physiology, pathology and surgery of the thyroid gland

### U.S. PRESIDENTS

**1897–1901** President William McKinley, *Republican*
**1897–1899** Vice President Garret A. Hobart
**1901** Vice President Theodore Roosevelt
**1901–1909** President Theodore Roosevelt, *Republican*
**1905–1909** Vice President Charles W. Fairbanks
**1909–1913** President William Howard Taft, *Republican*
**1909–1912** Vice President James S. Sherman

### SITES OF THE OLYMPIC GAMES

**1900** SUMMER  Paris, France
WINTER  *Not yet held*
**1904** SUMMER  St. Louis, Missouri
WINTER  *Not yet held*
**1908** SUMMER  London, England
WINTER  *Not yet held*

### KENTUCKY DERBY

**1900** Lieutenant Gibson
**1901** His Eminence
**1902** Alan-a-Dale
**1903** Judge Himes
**1904** Elwood
**1905** Agile
**1906** Sir Huon
**1907** Pink Star
**1908** Stone Street
**1909** Wintergreen

### WIMBLEDON CHAMPIONS

**1900** MEN Reggie F. Doherty
WOMEN Blanche Bingley Hillyard
**1901** MEN Arthur W. Gore
WOMEN Charlotte Cooper Sterry
**1902** MEN H. Laurie Doherty
WOMEN Muriel Robb
**1903** MEN H. Laurie Doherty
WOMEN Dorothea Douglass
**1904** MEN H. Laurie Doherty
WOMEN Dorothea Douglass
**1905** MEN H. Laurie Doherty
WOMEN May Sutton
**1906** MEN H. Laurie Doherty
WOMEN Dorothea Douglass
**1907** MEN Norman E. Brookes
WOMEN May Sutton
**1908** MEN Arthur W. Gore
WOMEN Charlotte Cooper Sterry
**1909** MEN Arthur W. Gore
WOMEN Dora Boothby

### WORLD SERIES CHAMPIONS

**1900** *Not yet played*
**1901** *Not yet played*
**1902** *Not yet played*
**1903** Boston Pilgrims defeat Pittsburgh Pirates
**1904** *Not played*
**1905** New York Giants defeat Philadelphia Athletics
**1906** Chicago White Sox defeat Chicago Cubs
**1907** Chicago Cubs defeat Detroit Tigers
**1908** Chicago Cubs defeat Detroit Tigers
**1909** Pittsburgh Pirates defeat Detroit Tigers